SPORTS HE

Tony
Hawk

Read all of the books in this exciting,
action-packed biography series!

Barry Bonds

Tim Duncan

Lou Gehrig

Mia Hamm

Tony Hawk

Michael Jordan

Michelle Kwan

Mickey Mantle

Shaquille O'Neal

Jackie Robinson

Babe Ruth

Ichiro Suzuki

SPORTS HEROES AND LEGENDS

Tony Hawk

by Edgar Greene

BARNES
& NOBLE
BOOKS

NEW YORK

To Stephanie and Todd, the cheer squad

Cover photographs:
Top: © David Leeds/Getty Images
Bottom: © Tom Hauck/Getty Images

Barnes & Noble Publishing, Inc.
122 Fifth Avenue
New York, NY 10011

ISBN 0-7607-3216-7

Printed in the United States of America

05 06 07 08 MCH 11 10 9 8 7 6 5 4 3

Written by Lisa Papademetriou

Sports Heroes and Legends™ is a trademark of
Barnes & Noble Publishing, Inc.

Contents

Riding the Asphalt

So, you probably think that skateboarding is a superkewl, brand-new sport that's only been around for a few years, right? Think again. The truth is, kids have been rolling around on wheels attached to wooden boards since the early 1900s. Of course, these weren't the sophisticated skateboards covered in cool graphics that you see today. They were homemade contraptions, put together with a two-by-four and a roller skate that had been sawed in half. At the time roller skates were made with metal wheels, which gave a rough ride and were notorious for their inability to grip the road. The smallest bump or pebble would send a would-be skateboarder flying. Still, for years, thousands of kids wheeled around happily on their handmade boards. No one thought of selling a commercial skateboard for almost sixty years!

The first manufactured skateboards appeared in stores in 1959. The Little Red Roller Derby Skateboard had steel wheels attached to a supernarrow four-and-a-half-inch-wide plywood board. In the early 1960s surfing was beginning to rise as a popular sport, and when the waves were bad, many surfers practiced their moves on land, using skateboards. The early sixties also saw two innovations in skateboarding—clay wheels and double-action trucks. Trucks are the part of the skateboard that fastens the axles and wheels to the actual "board" of the skateboard, and the double-action trucks made turning much easier. Meanwhile the clay wheels offered a much smoother ride than metal.

In 1963 Larry Stevenson formed a skateboarding team to promote his new professional skateboard design, which was shaped to look like a surfboard. Stevenson was the publisher of *Surf Guide,* and his company, Makaha, also sponsored the first skateboarding contest that year in Hermosa, California. The skateboarding team and the contest helped publicize the sport, and in 1965 the first ever National Skateboard Championships were aired on ABC's *Wide World of Sports.* A photograph of female skateboarder Pat McGee doing a handstand on a skateboard even appeared on the cover of *Life* magazine.

But later that fall, skateboarding's popularity suddenly slammed (in skateboard talk, that means it took a serious dive). The public was upset by reckless riding—over 50 million boards had been sold over the previous three years, and a lot of kids were getting hurt. Although the clay wheels on manufactured boards were a significant improvement over the metal wheels of the homemade boards, they were still rough on riders and provided very little traction. As former skater Jim Muir said in the documentary *Dogtown and Z-Boys*, "Any crack in the sidewalk was a hazard unto your health." Twenty cities even went so far as to ban skateboards, and soon the sport had virtually disappeared.

But some people never gave up on skateboarding, despite the hard times. Larry Stevenson was one of these diehards. He went back to the drawing board—literally—and came up with a skateboard design that had a brand-new feature: the kicktail. This design allowed a skater to press down on the rear of the board and use his body to make sharp turns, radically improving maneuverability. Then in the early 1970s a man named Frank Nasworthy developed a urethane wheel for skateboards. The new wheels were durable and gripped asphalt unbelievably well. "It was almost like a four-wheel drive now, where the car would just grab the ground and you could really, really make hard turns. It was the whole beginning of what skateboarding is today, period," said Bob Biniak, former member of the legendary Zephyr skate team. All of a sudden skateboarding took off again.

Although skateboarding was mostly dead in the late 1960s, there was one neighborhood in which it was thriving. The rough neighborhood of Dogtown, in Santa Monica, California, was a haven for surfers who also liked to practice skating in their free

In the 1960s skateboard prices ranged from $1.29 to $15.

time. And once skating resurfaced in the seventies, these Dogtown skaters led the way in creating moves that are the basis of skating as we know it today.

Jeff Ho, Skip Engblom, and Craig Stecyk started up a surfing team to promote their surfboard manufacturing company, called Zephyr, in Dogtown. When the waves were low, the Zephyr surf team would practice their moves on skateboards down the hill behind the surfboard shop. "Skateboarding was just an extension of our surfing," explained former Zephyr skater Allen Sarlo. In 1973 two members of the team showed Engblom the new urethane wheels, which were known as Cadillac Wheels. Engblom started carrying the wheels in the shop, and soon Zephyr was manufacturing skateboards as well as surfboards. Soon their surf team morphed into a skateboarding team with an aggressive style of skating that took surfing moves from the waves to the asphalt.

The first skateboarding contest that the Zephyr team entered was the 1975 Skateboard Championships in Del Mar, California, sponsored by Bahne Skateboards. Until then skateboarding competitors utilized a stiff, upright skating style that had been popular in the early sixties and performed tricks like handstands to win contests. But the moment that the Z-Boys took the stage, people could tell that they were different. The Zephyr team's style was much more fluid and fast, and the Z-Boys skated low to the ground. In the end the Zephyr team's only female member, Peggy Oki, took first place in women's freestyle, and the team's Jay Adams and Tony Alva took third and fourth place in junior men's freestyle, respectively.

❝The Zephyr team had guys with all different styles and really sparked a revolution.**❞**

—TONY HAWK

In the late seventies California experienced a severe drought. As a result of strict water restrictions, backyard pools across the area were drained. But the Z-Boys didn't see these empty pools as useless concrete holes in the ground—they saw nothing but an opportunity to skateboard on smooth, unused terrain, and vert pool skating was born. In 1977 Zephyr skaters began to do aerials out of the pool, and once again skateboarding reached a new stage of evolution.

The Z-Boys read like a roll call of seventies skateboarding legends, including Tony Alva, Jay Adams, and Stacy Peralta. Craig

Stecyk began writing articles about the Z-Boys for *SkateBoarder* magazine. Suddenly the Z-Boys were famous, and their style was changing the face of skateboarding across the country. Unfortunately, Zephyr encountered some business difficulties. Eventually the team broke up and Zephyr closed up shop. But that didn't stop the Z-Boys' involvement in skateboarding. Tony Alva started his own skateboarding company. So did Stacy Peralta, who cofounded Powell and Peralta with George Powell. And so did Jim Muir, who cofounded Dogtown Skates.

In the mid-1960s 50 million skateboards were made. In 2002 it is estimated that 11 million people own and ride skateboards, and over a million people begin the sport each year.

In 1976 the first skateboard park, Skatboard (the misspelling was intentional) City in Port Orange, Florida, was built. The park had concrete bowls in which skateboarders could practice tricks. Now instead of skating on the flat street, skateboarders were practicing on curved surfaces, and suddenly skateboarding went from being a horizontal to a vertical sport. The Dogtown label began marketing decks with cool graphics, and many other board makers followed their lead.

Not only was the style of skateboarding evolving, the boards themselves were continuing to morph and change. In 1975 Jim Muir—the former Z-Boy—and his partner, Wes Humpston, began making their own skateboards. Humpston had studied art in school and began adding graffiti-style drawings to the bottom of his skateboards. After a while everyone wanted one of his Dogtown decks. Not only were these boards beautiful, Humpston and Muir made them wider than the standard size. The wider decks were more stable, especially on vert surfaces. Other skateboard companies hopped on the bandwagon, and soon the standard size for decks went from between six and seven inches to over nine.

But if there was a single skateboarder who had the greatest influence on the progression of the sport, that skater had to be Alan Gelfand. Alan, whose nickname was "Ollie," invented the ollie pop and the ollie aerial, which are the foundation of almost every skateboarding trick today. In 1977 Stacy Peralta went to Florida to visit skateparks and saw Gelfand pop his board with his back foot. Gelfand and Peralta became fast friends, and when Peralta cofounded Powell and Peralta, he quickly called Gelfand and asked him to be on the Powell skateboarding team, which later became known as the Bones Brigade. When Jim Cassimus photographed Gelfand performing the ollie on a ramp for *SkateBoarder* magazine, the trick transformed skateboarding almost immediately. And things have never been the same.

The year 1981 saw the publication of *Thrasher* magazine, followed quickly by *Transworld Skateboarding* in 1984. The Great Desert Ramp Battle, the first large professional ramp contest, was held in Palmdale, California. And skateboarding was ready for yet another revolution. Until the mid-1980s skateboarders had competed mainly in two categories—vert and freestyle. Vert took place in pools and on ramps and was an exciting skate style to watch because of the aerial tricks involved. Freestyle skateboarding was performed on flat surfaces, and the tricks were choreographed to music, much the way ice skating or gymnastics routines are performed. It was less exciting to watch, and eventually the style faded away. But in the eighties something new and exciting rose to take the place of freestyle—a skate style that combined the outlandish tricks of vert skating with flat surfaces: street skating. Instead of pools and half pipes, street skaters used park benches, handrails, banisters, and almost any kind of street furniture as platforms for their tricks.

At the end of that decade, skateboarding was popular, but it wasn't mainstream. Many people still feared that the sport was dangerous and mistrusted skaters, who had a reputation as being wild and reckless. The new era of skating needed a new face to promote the sport and take it to the public. Someone who was approachable but who could also perform the sickest skating moves ever.

Tony Hawk was the perfect skater for the job.

Chapter One

Just 500 More!

Tony Hawk has always been passionate—some might even say obsessive—about skateboarding. When he first discovered the sport, other skaters' tricks fascinated him. Tony would watch skateboarders practicing at Oasis Skatepark, and whenever anyone would pull off a new trick, Tony would immediately try it. Sometimes skaters got angry, thinking that he was trying to show off and prove that he was better than they were. But Tony wasn't really trying to outdo the other skaters—he was just trying to learn new things and outdo himself.

According to his best-selling autobiography, *Hawk: Occupation: Skateboarder,* Tony's perfectionist streak was in fine form the day he learned to do inverts. An invert is when you ride up to the edge of the bowl and balance yourself upside down on one hand while holding on to your board with the other. It's a difficult trick, and Tony was only eleven years old at the time.

But he was determined to do an invert. He knew that he could get it if he just worked hard enough.

66When I skate, I never go halfway. If I don't do my best, it eats at me.99

—TONY HAWK

One evening Tony's father arrived to pick him up for dinner while Tony was practicing his frontside rocks. At the time, Tony worshiped a skater named Eddie Elguera, and the frontside rock was Elguera's signature move. A frontside rock is a move in which you bring the front wheels of your skateboard up over the lip of the pool or half pipe, then rock the rear of your board and kickturn back down into the bowl. Today a frontside rock is considered a basic skateboard move, but at the time that Tony was learning to do them, even professional skaters were having difficulty with them. Tony worked on his frontside rocks for about an hour and a half while his father waited patiently for him to finish. Finally Frank Hawk had had enough. He strode into the bowl and told Tony to hurry up.

But Tony had only just begun—now he was ready to try inverts. He fell on a few tries but didn't want to give up. "He could never leave a park until he had perfected a trick," Tony's

11

brother, Steve Hawk, once told reporters. Still, his father was getting impatient. Tony begged and pleaded for a few more tries, but Frank Hawk insisted that they leave. Tony refused, so his father grabbed him and dragged him out of the bowl. "[Tony] would kick and scream, 'If I do this trick five hundred more times, I can get it!'" Nancy Hawk, his mother, later confirmed.

Tony's childhood hero was Evel Knievel, a famous daredevil motorcyclist.

Tony has always been full of surprises. His mother was forty-three years old and his father was forty-five when Tony was born at Sharp Hospital in San Diego. They already had three children: Lenore, who was twenty-one, Patricia, who was eighteen, and Steve, who was twelve. Nancy and Frank hadn't expected any more children.

Tony's father had a heart attack when Tony's mother was five months pregnant. Once Frank had recovered, Nancy joked to her friends that Frank had gone into cardiac arrest when she'd told him that she was expecting Tony. "I told him, 'Don't dare leave me after getting me like this,'" Nancy kidded. Nancy and Frank Hawk always relied on their sense of humor to get them through difficult times. Frank lost his job as a small-appliances salesman shortly after his heart attack, and Nancy was going to school as well as working full-time while raising her kids. Things weren't easy for the Hawks, but Tony remembers his childhood as a happy one—especially since he had two parents who doted on him . . . maybe a little too much. "My brother and sisters had moved out by the time I was a kid, so it was like being an only child," Tony later admitted.

Tony's parents were never very strict, and they always supported their children's interests, encouraging them to do well in whatever they tried. Tony's brother, Steve, surfed, and Frank would drive him to the beach every morning and watch while Steve practiced his moves before school. "I probably spent too much time with the kids," Frank later confessed. "But if they were into something that wasn't harmful, well, then we tried to support it and open doors."

Tony was a very active child who drove himself hard. Maybe some of that drive came from his father, who had a military background. Frank Hawk had been a navy pilot during both World War II and the Korean War, and he was highly decorated for his service. But as a young child, Tony's drive wasn't nearly as disciplined as his father's—Tony was prone to sudden emotional outbursts. He was also very competitive and grew angry when he played a card or board game that he thought he couldn't win. One time, at the age of six, Tony's mom took him swimming. The pool was Olympic size, and when Tony saw that huge ocean of sparkling, clear water, he decided that he would challenge himself. He wanted to swim the entire length of it . . . without taking a breath. Naturally, he couldn't do it—a six-year-old's lungs are too small to hold enough air for such a long trip underwater. Still, Tony was furious with himself, angry that he had "failed."

Tony's parents admired his determination, but they worried about the fact that their son became frustrated and angry so easily. Also, Tony had trouble sitting still in class. His body was always moving, and no one could seem to make sense of it. "I was impatient and uncooperative," Tony later recalled. "I'm sure it had something to do with my diet—soda, candy, ice cream all the time. I'd drink Cokes until I had a sugar buzz. If I were growing up now, teachers would probably say I had attention deficit disorder," a common learning disability.

But Nancy Hawk had her own suspicions as to why Tony was so difficult. She thought that her son wasn't being challenged enough in school and that his behavior reflected the fact that he was, well, bored. She had always known that Tony was intelligent. He had been a big fan of *Sesame Street* for years, and by the time he was five, Tony read so well that his kindergarten teacher often asked him to read aloud to the class. He also began working ahead of the class in math. So when Tony's behavior began to get out of hand in the second grade, Nancy Hawk had the school give her son an IQ test. She was, perhaps, the only person who wasn't surprised when Tony's IQ turned out to be a superhigh 144. Her whirling dervish of a son was way smart, and the problem was that his gifted brain wanted his eight-year-old body to do things that he wasn't ready for yet.

❝*Tony seizes the thin line that separates genius from insanity and ties it in knots.***❞**

—POWELL AND PERALTA AD,
APPEARING IN THE MARCH 1984 ISSUE OF *THRASHER* MAGAZINE

Tony was placed in advanced classes in reading and math. Although he eventually decided to return to his grade level in reading, the extra challenge in math kept Tony's mind active. He also learned to play the violin and joined Little League baseball and basketball, which his father coached. But Tony was never all that interested in team sports. When he didn't perform up to his own high expectations, he always felt that he had let the entire team down. It was a lot of pressure for an eight-year-old, and Tony hated it. But his parents thought that the physical activity was helpful in managing Tony's energy level, so they encouraged him to stick with sports. Of course, sports did end up changing Tony's life and attitude forever. He just had to find the right one.

Chapter Two

Hitting the Deck

One day, when Tony was nine, his older brother, Steve, came home from college for a visit. Steve had been studying journalism in Santa Barbara, and Tony's parents had recently moved to Tierrasanta. Steve had always been interested in surfing, and as a result he had a "sidewalk surfboard" that he practiced on when the waves were flat. On this particular visit Steve dug his old, beat-up fiberglass Bahne skateboard out of the garage and showed Tony how to use it. "My older brother, Steve, gave me my first board," Tony recalled. "He said, 'You should try this.'"

Tony didn't quite show himself to be "naturally gifted" with the board. In fact, he couldn't figure out how to make the thing turn! He would just roll forward until he came to an obstacle, then step off the board, turn it around, step back on, and roll away in the opposite direction. It wasn't exactly loads of fun. Tony got bored with it pretty quickly, until Steve took the time to show Tony how to carve (turn in a wide arc, with all four wheels on the ground) and perform a kickturn. Tony thought this was sort of fun, but it wasn't really a case of love at first sight. Steve gave Tony the skateboard, and Tony threw it back into the garage. He took it out once in a while but didn't think about it much.

When Tony started skateboarding, he was so small that he had to wear elbow pads on his knees!

A few months later Tony began to hang out with a bunch of kids who were interested in skateboarding. Tony still didn't take skateboarding seriously, but he went along when his friends rolled around the neighborhood. Ever eager to support his son's interests, Frank Hawk built a small ramp in the driveway for Tony and bought him a Sims skateboard. But it wasn't until the following year—fifth grade—that Tony fell in love with skateboarding . . . or at least, with a skatepark.

Tony had always admired Oasis Skatepark from afar. It was a fifteen-minute drive from where he lived, and Tony could see it from the freeway when his father drove past it. The year was 1978, and skateboarding was peaking once again. Oasis had two large pools, a snake run, a reservoir, a flat area for beginners, and a half pipe. It was a skater's dream, and it was almost always packed. One day the mother of one of Tony's friends took the boys to the skatepark, and from that moment on, Tony was hooked.

❝I'm usually skating for fun. Practice is 'training' by default.**❞**

—TONY HAWK

A number of great skaters used the concrete at Oasis. In fact, Tony's first real skateboard was a Dave Andrecht model— and Dave Andrecht practiced at Oasis. There were plenty of people to look up to and learn from, and Tony watched them all. Tony couldn't get enough of Oasis, and he did everything he could to get back there. He didn't have enough money for the admission, so he got a paper route. By then Steve had graduated from college and was working at a paper nearby. Tony's dad volunteered to take Tony to the skatepark a couple of times a week, and soon skating became Tony's favorite sport.

To tell the truth, Tony had never been all that interested in baseball or basketball, even though he played on teams. Part of the problem was that he was always hard on himself and hated to feel that any mistake he made would let down the entire team. But the other part was that Tony didn't like being bossed around. Skateboarding suited his personality better. "I just liked being freer, not having to submit to some practice schedule of repetitive passing and shooting, not having to rely on all of the players to do well," he later said. "There's a lot of practice and repetition in skateboarding, but it's at your own pace. It's not someone telling you what to do."

Tony gave up baseball and basketball . . . but he didn't give up learning to play the violin.

It wasn't easy for Tony to tell his father that he didn't want to play team sports anymore—Frank was the coach of the basketball team and had just been elected Little League president. But when Tony finally admitted that he preferred skateboarding, Frank didn't even seem surprised. After all, Tony had been showing up to basketball practice still wearing his skating knee pads. He realized that his son had found his sport, and he wasn't going to force Tony to do anything he didn't want to do. Besides, skateboarding had already had a positive influence on Tony—his personality was less intense and his drive more focused. "We were really happy he was taking his energy out on that skateboard instead of us," Nancy Hawk later told a reporter.

As Tony became more comfortable on his board, skateboarding grew from a love to an obsession. First he learned to do rock 'n' rolls, in which you go up one side of the bowl, hit a kickturn, and go back down facing the other direction. Next Tony progressed to airs, tricks in which a skateboarder zooms past the top of a ramp and is in the air for a moment before skating back down the ramp. At the time most skateboarders early-grabbed into their airs. That meant that they grabbed the board before they left the ground and held on to it while they were in the air. But Tony was too small to early-grab— he couldn't get enough momentum to keep himself airborne. Tony was determined to find a solution, and he did—instead of early-grabbing, he ollied into his airs. Tony was committed to improving as much as he could. "He was a skinny little kid, all padded up," recalled Grant Brittain, former manager of Del Mar

----

❝When he started getting good at skating, it changed his personality. Finally, he was doing something that he was satisfied with.❞

—STEVE HAWK

Skatepark and world-famous skateboard photographer. "There were a lot of kids back then who got dropped off as a baby-sitting service. . . . Tony just kept busy, skating."

The next year, at the age of eleven, Tony decided to enter a skateboarding contest, even though the whole idea made him incredibly nervous. Tony's first contest was held at Oasis, so at least he knew the terrain, but the thought didn't comfort Tony much—he was too busy psyching himself out, picturing all the ways he could embarrass himself.

When Tony arrived at the skatepark, the place was mobbed with skaters and spectators. At the time the major amateur association that held competitions was the Association of Skatepark Owners (ASPO). The rules stated that all entrants had to write down a detailed account of their planned routine and hand it to the judges before their turn. Competitors were restricted to performing those tricks that were on their lists. By the time Tony's turn came, he was so nervous that he was a complete wreck. He did horribly—messing up on even his easiest tricks. In fact, he did so poorly that he didn't stay to see how he'd placed. Tony was disappointed with himself and how he had skated, but he didn't give up on skateboarding. In fact, Tony's failures usually only prompted him to try harder. And that's why Tony kept skating after his first lousy contest.

Tony began entering every skateboarding contest he heard about. When a contest was at a skatepark other than Oasis, he would go to the other park and practice on it beforehand. Then he would go home and plan his run, making up a list of the tricks he planned to do and drawing a map of where they would happen in the bowl. Tony also invented a trick, the "backside varial," in which he would go up the ramp with the tail of his board facing forward, rotate the board 180 degrees in the air, and land going back down the ramp, also with his tail in the lead. Tony usually saved this trick for last so that the judges would be left with that image in their minds. "Tony's very creative," Steve later recalled. "But the thing about Tony is he's always had the presence to hold off his best tricks until the end. He has brought strategy to the sport."

Tony got better and better, and by the end of the year he entered a contest and won his age group. Shortly after that, he was given a place on the Oasis Skatepark team.

His skateboarding career was just getting started.

At Tony's first contest, there were over a hundred competitors registered in his age division alone.

Chapter Three

Dogtown

By the time Tony was eleven, skateboarding's popularity was taking a dive. Most skaters were leaving the sport without a backward glance. But Tony's interest just kept growing. As Tony later put it, "I skated when there was nothing going on." He couldn't skate enough. Despite the fact that many skateparks were closing down, Oasis Skatepark stayed open, and Tony kept skating there. He also skated every day before

Tony has a brilliant smile, but his front two teeth are fake as a result of a skateboarding injury.

classes started, practicing on the curb outside the school building. Sometimes the principal of the school would even come outside and watch him!

Because interest in skateboarding was dying, many skate companies were having a hard time making ends meet. One of those companies was Dogtown Skates. Tony's dad knew that Dogtown wanted to save money, so he invited Denise Barter, the manager of the Dogtown team, to stay with them while she was in town for a contest at Oasis. When she left, Denise thanked Frank and gave Tony a new Dogtown deck. Tony thought that the skateboard was cool, but he had no idea that Denise had her eye on him. When Dogtown came back for another contest, she asked Tony to join the team. Tony was officially sponsored, which meant that he got a new skateboard and trucks and that Dogtown would now pay his expenses to compete in skateparks all over California.

Tony wasn't even thirteen when he started skating for Powell . . . but he skated for the Bones Brigade for the next thirteen years!

Tony didn't think that his sponsorship meant that much—he was just happy to have another free skateboard. But one day, when he was skating at Oasis, Tony slammed into Dave Andrecht. Tony took a bad fall. He was bruised and scraped, and he did what any eleven-year-old would do when he's just been scratched up by a bunch of concrete—he started to cry. "You can't cry now," Andrecht told him. "You're sponsored." That was when Tony realized that although the sponsorship hadn't really changed his life, it had changed how other skaters saw him. Suddenly he was in a whole new league.

He was happy to be on the team, though, because a couple of his skater friends were already on it. At school many of the kids treated Tony as an outcast because skating was suddenly so unpopular. This treatment lasted for most of Tony's school career. "I just didn't relate to anyone," Tony later recalled. "I never went to a single school function. . . . I was going to school because I had to." But on the team Tony had people to practice and talk about skateboarding with. He felt like he belonged.

Skateparks and skateboard companies weren't the only businesses hurting from the sudden lack of interest in the sport— the Association of Skatepark Owners also went out of business. Tony's dad saw that there was an urgent need for an organization to organize competitions for skateboarders, and so in 1980 he founded the California Amateur Skatepark League (CASL). Frank

Hawk drew on his experience as a Little League president in setting up the CASL. The CASL organized competitions, and skateboard manufacturers gave the CASL money to display their logos at events. Frank thought that it was important to set up an organization that seemed fair and impartial, so he made sure that the CASL had a uniform set of competition rules and standards for judging. Frank also realized that many parents were uncomfortable with skateboarding's dangerous image. He knew that skateboarding was doomed unless parents were behind it—after all, who would buy all of the equipment for the kids?—so he required that skaters wear safety equipment in competitions. Tony's mom got involved in the CASL, too, as a scorer at competitions.

Tony felt a little strange competing in contests that his father had arranged. He worried that other skaters would think that his father had arranged the CASL only for his son's benefit. As Tony's brother, Steve, once said, "At first, Tony was embarrassed about winning competitions set up by my father, scored by judges who answered to my father. Every victory was tainted." Sometimes Tony would cope with his embarrassment by ignoring his father at competitions. "We didn't talk during contests," Tony remembered. It was uncomfortable for a while, but eventually Tony got used to seeing his father at the skatepark. Tony later said that his father "was the guy who stepped in and got organized skateboarding started when no one else would."

> **❝**[Tony] was performing on a stage my father had built.**❞**
>
> —STEVE HAWK

Tony's team, Dogtown, sold skateboarding decks, so they liked to have a number of skaters place highly in the rankings at competitions. Generally speaking, if a team's skaters do well, their products sell well. But that wasn't always the case in the early eighties, when Tony was skating for Dogtown. The truth was, at that moment in skateboarding history, nothing was really selling very well.

Still, Tony took skateboarding very seriously, and he was willing to suffer if it meant that he would improve. One day, when Tony was skating at Oasis, he slammed on a simple trick and knocked himself unconscious. Eventually a fellow skater found Tony and called his parents, who met Tony at a nearby hospital. The doctor kept giving Tony's parents suspicious looks as he examined Tony. Then he started asking questions. After all, Tony's body was covered with scrapes and bruises, and the doctor wanted to know where they had come from. After a while Tony realized that the doctor thought his parents had been abusing him! Tony and his dad explained that Tony practiced on his skateboard all the time and that he often fell and hurt himself. It took a while, but eventually they managed to convince the doctor that Tony's injuries really were from slamming.

Luckily all of that pain finally paid off. At the end of the first year of the organization the CASL awarded Tony a trophy for "most improved skater." Of course, with all of the people who had suddenly stopped skating, the competition wasn't that tough!

When Tony was in the seventh grade, his family moved to Cardiff, California, which was near Del Mar Skatepark. Del Mar was run by Grant Brittain, who later became the photo editor of *Transworld Skateboarding* magazine and an internationally famous skateboard photographer. At first, Tony didn't like Del Mar very much. He had skated there in the past—it was only about a half-hour drive from his old house—and had discovered that there was a flaw in one of the pools. Still, Tony didn't have much of a choice, and eventually he found that Del Mar had a great community of skaters, even if it didn't have the world's smoothest bowls.

One day, when Tony was skating in a competition at Upland, former Zephyr skater Stacy Peralta walked up to him and asked him how Dogtown was treating him. Tony was shocked, to put it mildly—Peralta had been skateboarding world champion in 1977 and was a skateboarding legend. Peralta had already started his skateboarding company, Powell and Peralta, and their team had some incredible skaters, including Jay Adams, Steve Caballero, and Mike McGill.

So when Tony found himself talking to Peralta at Upland, he didn't know what to say. He had no idea that Peralta had been watching his skating for a while and thought that Tony had talent.

Both Steve Caballero and Mike McGill would eventually have an impact on skateboarding history. Steve Caballero was the first to skate a 360-degree ollie, which he called the Caballerial. Mike McGill invented the 540 McTwist.

A few months later Dogtown Skates went under, and Peralta called Tony to ask him if he would be interested in a sponsorship with Powell and Peralta. Peralta also offered a sponsorship to Tony's best friend at the time, Kevin Straab. Kevin thought Powell was all that, so Tony agreed to join, too. Tony wasn't even thirteen years old, and he was already on his second sponsorship!

One of the longtime members of the Powell team was Ray "Bones" Rodriguez. Rodriguez skated on a board that had a distinctive graphic: a skeleton holding a sword. Skulls and skeletons became the Powell team's trademark, and eventually the team became known as the Bones Brigade. Tony was by far the youngest member of the Bones Brigade, and the other members of the team always encouraged him and rooted him on in competitions. But Tony was intimidated by the new level he had reached in skateboarding. He was used to competing against other amateur skaters from California. But Powell participated in national contests, where the competition was extreme.

For a long time Tony wasn't happy with the way he skated for Powell. He really respected everyone on his team and hated the feeling that he was letting them down when he didn't skate well. It probably didn't help that Tony—an eighty-pound twelve-year-old—was comparing himself to his teammates, some of whom were as old as eighteen and already legends in skate-boarding. But that was Tony—always tough on himself.

Even though Tony wasn't happy with the way he was skating for Powell, he preferred skating to anything else. Starting in eighth grade, Tony attended Serra High School, a rough place where skateboarding was thought to be about as cool as grandma's hair net. Tony was regularly picked on for his awkward, skinny physique. But that just made him more determined to do well in competitions. "I'd take the bus to the skatepark after school every day, and my dad would pick me up at night," Tony later recalled. "I'd skate for two or three hours, stop, hang out at the park, then skate again for another two or three hours."

Tony had high standards, and he was going to do whatever it took to live up to them.

Chapter Four

Going Pro

These days, being a professional skater can mean big business. In 1998 there were about 350 professional skateboarders in the United States. While most pros don't make much money, the top stars—of which there are about ten—can earn hundreds of thousands of dollars a year. Skateboard equipment and clothing companies are willing to pay top dollar to have professional skateboarders display their logos or endorse their products. Also, competitions can mean hefty bucks. In 2002 the total prize money for winners of the X Games totaled nearly $1 million. And in the 2002 Gravity Games, Eric Koston took home $23,000 for his first-place finish in the Street category. Not bad for a total of three minutes' work!

But in 1982 professional skateboarders didn't even dream of getting rich. Prize money was usually either puny or non-existent—typically a first-place win would pay about $150, second place would pay $100, and third place $50. Sometimes skaters simply competed for new equipment. Skateboarding companies couldn't afford to pay a large number of skateboarders to display their logos—there just wasn't enough money to go around—so there simply weren't that many pro skaters. Besides, back in the early eighties, the skaters who *did* turn pro still competed against amateurs all the time. There wasn't much of a distinction between them.

At the age of fifteen, Tony was already internationally famous—he appeared on a Japanese TV show called *Miracle Children of the World*!

That's why Tony didn't think turning pro was any big deal. One day he and the rest of the Bones Brigade were at a local skating contest, and as Tony filled out his entry form, Stacy Peralta asked him if he wanted to turn pro. Tony shrugged and put a check mark next to the word *professional* on the form. That was all there was to it.

Tony placed third in his first professional competition—not bad for a fourteen-year-old. But the contest didn't give any prize money for third place. And Tony didn't exactly cause a major splash in the world of skateboarding, either. . . . There were less than twenty spectators in the stands that day. Going pro had hardly changed his life.

Tony did even better in his second pro contest than he had in his first. The contest was held at Del Mar—and Tony came in first place! Tony later said in his autobiography that he felt that contest was important not because he won, but because it symbolized a shift in skateboarding. In the past raw, aggressive skating was what won contests. But the contest at Del Mar showed that innovative tricks could win, too. It was the beginning of a new breed of skateboarding.

But something else had started to change in the world of skateboarding—the image. Skateboarding had always had something of a hard-core punk image. Loud rock music often blared at the skateparks or accompanied skaters as they performed their tricks at competitions. But in the early eighties New Wave started to appear on the scene. Tony began to wear long shorts and bright T-shirts. His blond hair was clipped short in back while the front flopped into his face—a hairdo that was known to skateboarders as the "McSqueeb." Today people might look back at

---

66_His style was so different, so creative . . . so dangerous._**99**

—STACY PERALTA

Tony's appearance and laugh at his early eighties/Duran Duran style, but back then, it was considered seriously cutting edge. Eventually other skaters started to imitate Tony's look—one barbershop even started advertising "Tony Hawk Haircuts."

Even though Tony started out strong as a professional, it wasn't as though he ruled skateboarding right away. He placed tenth in his third pro competition and sixth in his fourth. He had a mild comeback in his fifth contest, where he placed fourth. Tony didn't really mind losing, but he was furious because he felt that he wasn't skating as well as he could . . . or should.

One day a teacher confiscated Tony's skateboard and wouldn't give it back until his father came to pick it up. When Frank Hawk arrived at the school, he was furious— at the teacher! After all, Frank was Tony's biggest fan.

To top it off, not everyone was wild about Tony's skateboarding style. From the beginning Tony had always ollied into his airs instead of early-grabbing, and he invented a lot of his own tricks. Tony used his feet to launch himself off the lip of the ramp, and he did a lot of flip tricks, which were derived from flat-ground, freestyle skateboarding. The old-school vert skateboarders called Tony a circus skater. One skateboarder named

Micke Alba even called Tony the biggest "cheat" in skateboarding in an interview with a magazine.

When Tony read that, his feelings were hurt. It wasn't like he was trying to cheat. The irony was that Tony actually *wanted* to be an old-school skater. If he could have skated powerful carves, he would have. But although Tony had gotten taller, he hadn't gained much weight. If he wanted to catch air, he had to ollie. And because he was kind of scrawny, his complicated tricks often made people uncomfortable—they thought that he was going to hurt himself and were amazed when he survived. His "cheating," "circus" style wasn't intentional; it was the only style he could do.

Going pro wasn't the only change for Tony in 1982—he also transferred to a new school, Torrey Pines High School. It was in a much nicer area, offered independent studies classes (which Tony used to put together a skateboarding curriculum), and had a principal who liked skateboarding. Finally Tony had found a school where he felt like he fit in.

The following year, in 1983, Frank Hawk decided to take what he had done for California with the CASL to the national level. He started the National Skateboard Association (NSA), the first circuit for professional skateboarders. It had the support of all of the major skateboard companies and offered a uniform ranking system for pros.

> **❝**Skating is about being an individual, but at the same time, it's about having a community and finding a common bond with other people.**❞**
>
> —TONY HAWK

This was both good and bad for Tony. As a professional skateboarder, Tony realized that the NSA was important—it would bring national attention to skateboarding. But Tony worried more than ever that other skaters would feel that the contests were rigged because his dad had organized them—especially since he was already labeled a "cheat." Also, Frank Hawk's military background didn't help matters. He would yell at skaters who broke the rules, and he sometimes went overboard looking out for his son. As Frank Hawk later told *Sports Illustrated,* "I used to embarrass [Tony]. If I thought he was being defaulted, I'd mouth off. If he got pushed aside on a run, I'd tell the kid, 'Do it again, you'll have to deal with me.' I think now he would have rather had me out of it."

It also didn't help matters that the first NSA competition was at Del Mar and Tony placed first. Rumors began to fly that the contest had been rigged. Tony wasn't happy about that, but he realized that the NSA was important to a lot of people, not just him. In the end, he decided to suck it up. It took a while, but eventually the skaters got used to Tony's parents. And the Hawks absolutely loved the skaters. They were now in their sixties, but they fed off the skateboarders' punk style and raw energy.

In 1983, thanks in part to the NSA, skateboarding's popularity began to grow . . . slowly. Stacy Peralta told Tony that Powell wanted to release a Tony Hawk pro model skateboard. Peralta told Tony to come up with a graphic for the board, so Tony asked one of his friends to draw a picture of a swooping hawk. Tony showed the image to the artist at Powell, who cleaned up the image and sent it off to be reproduced on the board. When Tony saw his new skateboard, he freaked. He had just given the artist the picture so that he would have an idea of what Tony wanted—he hadn't meant for it to be the final picture. After all, the friend who had drawn it for Tony was a good artist, but he was only fourteen! Unfortunately there was nothing that could be done about it. Tony was stuck with the board.

Tony was told that he would make eighty-five cents for each Tony Hawk model that was sold, but the swooping hawk design didn't exactly set the world on fire. When Tony received his first royalty check, it was for eighty-five cents, which meant that Powell had sold exactly one Tony Hawk skateboard. A few months later Tony got another check, this one for five times as much: $4.25. Unsurprisingly, Powell discontinued the board design soon afterward, and the Powell artist gave Tony a new graphic—a bird skull with an Iron Cross design in the background. Tony immediately began making money—between $500 and $1,000 a month. That's some serious bank for an early eighties fifteen-year-old. Eventually that design became Tony's most popular graphic ever.

That year Stacy Peralta began filming the *Bones Brigade Video Show,* a skateboarding video, to promote Powell's products. The Bones Brigade skated their best tricks for the video, and it sold like crazy—over 30,000 copies at a time when few people owned VCRs. The sales of Tony's skateboard went wild, and soon he was making $3,000 a month on the sales.

The Hawk was beginning to take flight.

As nice as it was to turn pro, Tony was far more excited by something else that happened in 1982—he made the cover of *Thrasher* magazine!

Chapter Five

Flying High

In November 1983 Tony competed in the Upland Turkey Shoot. The contest was held at the dreaded course that skaters called "the Badlands." Tony only came in fourth in the competition, but he didn't mind. His goal was to show everyone that he could skate well in a tough park, and he'd done that. Besides, the skaters who had taken the top three places ahead of him—Lance Mountain, Steve Caballero, and Mike McGill—were all on the Bones Brigade. The Powell team had swept the contest, which was great for the team.

Tony skated hard and practiced often. During the summer he competed in contests in the United States and Europe (in the early 1980s skateboarding was huge in England, France, Germany, and Sweden) and spent five weeks on the road with the Bones Brigade doing skateboarding demonstrations, or demos. By the end of the year he had placed sixth in one contest, taken fourth in two, and had won first place in three. When all the points were counted, Tony was named the first NSA world champion!

Of course, Tony wasn't too impressed with this honor. The truth was, the NSA gave the award to whoever had the greatest point total in a given year. Skaters were given a certain number of points for placing in contests. That meant that if you entered two contests and came in first, you wouldn't have as many points as someone who entered ten contests and always came in fourth. So Tony figured that he might have just entered more contests than anyone else. Still, there was no doubt about it— he was skating well, and people were starting to notice.

❝[Skaters] need each other for moral support.❞
—TONY HAWK

In 1984 street skating was just beginning to become popular. Tony's specialty had always been vert, but he entered a street contest in San Francisco and came in seventh place. Tony continued to compete in vert contests, skating better and better. He also spent more and more time doing demos over the weekends. At the end of 1984 Tony was named NSA champion—again.

In the fall of 1984 Tony made a friend who would have a big influence on his life. While he was in Fresno, California, to perform a demo, he met Cindy Dunbar. Cindy and Tony hit it off right away and became instant friends. When Tony had to return home, he and Cindy kept in touch by writing letters. At that point Tony definitely wasn't in love with Cindy, but he thought she was a very cool friend. He had no idea that she would one day become his wife.

Tony started 1985 off well—he won the first NSA contest of the year, which was held at Del Mar. Next up was a competition at the Badlands, and Tony was ready. Once again he really wanted to skate well at that park to prove to people that he was more than just a circus skater who only knew Del Mar. But Tony surprised even himself when he came in first at the Badlands! He had grown a lot as a skater . . . but he had also grown physically. At this point he was six feet tall and had gained some weight. Now, instead of looking like a scrawny little kid, he looked like an athlete, and he seemed to be more in command of his tricks.

Tony did get a chance to skate at Del Mar again, briefly, when he was cast as an extra in the movie *Thrashin'*, parts of which were shot at Del Mar.

That year Frank Hawk suffered a heart attack. Tony was terrified for his father, but Frank was a true fighter and was out of the hospital in a few days. And as soon as he was well, he went right back to running the NSA and bawling out skaters who didn't follow his rules. There was nothing Tony could do to stop him, so he decided to just let his dad do his thing. But the frightening experience definitely brought the two together. "I found out later in the minutes before the ambulance arrived, when [Tony] was feeling helpless, he really opened up to my dad," Steve Hawk later recalled. "Told him how much he loved him. How he was the greatest father. How he appreciated everything he had done."

66*People were blown away by the things he was doing back then.***99**
—STACY PERALTA

During the summer of 1986 Tony taught skateboarding at a summer camp in Sweden. Tony's schedule wasn't very demanding, and he didn't have as many distractions as he did at home, which left a lot of time to practice skateboarding. Tony used his time to practice new tricks and techniques and came back to the United States a stronger skater. That year the *Christian Science Monitor* reported, "Tony Hawk does things on a skateboard that many professional gymnasts, tumblers, divers, and acrobats might congratulate themselves for doing *off* a skateboard." All of a sudden the criticism of Tony's style dried up, and people were expressing awe at his skateboarding genius. In the same article Tony explained that "over the years, the [other skaters] have come to realize I got where I am by my talent, nothing else." Tony still saved his best trick for last in competitions—a 720, in which he somersaulted twice in the air and landed cleanly on the board. At the time Tony was the only skater who could pull that trick.

Meanwhile two years had passed since the release of the *Bones Brigade Video Show.* The video had been so popular that Stacy Peralta decided it was time to release a new one and began work on *Future Primitive.* Skateboarding's popularity was on a fast rise, and street skating was grabbing people's attention. *Future Primitive* was more sophisticated than the *Bones Brigade Video Show,* and it showcased how far the sport of skateboarding had come in a short time. It was tremendously successful, and Powell's skateboard sales skyrocketed. Tony—along with the rest of the Bones Brigade—began raking in as much as $7,000 a month. He had appeared in ads for Swatch watches and Mountain Dew and was earning money from those

The only job Tony was ever fired from was *Police Academy 4.* He was supposed to be David Spade's stunt double, but Tony was almost a foot too tall!

sponsorships. Not only that, but Tony was skating better than ever and took the NSA championship for the third time.

By the time Tony was a senior in high school, his hectic schedule meant that he had to miss a lot of school. To make matters worse, his parents had moved from Cardiff to Carlsbad, California, and now his commute to school was a grueling forty minutes each way. But even if he wasn't in danger of being elected class valedictorian, at least he was at the top of his game in skateboarding. He started winning contest after contest. Soon Tony had made so much money that his sister suggested he buy a house in Carlsbad. "He was out looking at homes and reading brochures the next day," Frank Hawk later recalled. His mom didn't want him to move out, but Tony wanted to be independent. Besides, his new house was only five minutes away from his parents' home—he could still go home for dinner whenever he wanted.

Tony was the first pro skateboarder to take first place in three contests in a row.

The summer after his senior year, Tony spent five weeks on tour with the Bones Brigade. When he returned home, he heard that Del Mar was closing down. Their insurance costs had gotten too high and they couldn't afford to keep the park open any longer. Tony, who had spent a lot of his skate time there, was devastated. He started skating at a friend's backyard ramp in Fallbrook, but it didn't feel the same. Tony's skateboarding clearly didn't suffer, however. At the end of 1986 he was NSA world champion *again*.

Powell released its next video, *The Search for Animal Chin*, in 1987. The video was shot at a park that featured a wooden W-shaped double half pipe, and people were amazed by the Bones Brigade's daredevil stunts, like flips (which are somersaults in which the skateboarder holds on to the board) and inverts. Tony recalled filming *The Search for Animal Chin* as one of his best memories of his time with the Bones Brigade. "We basically lived with each other for nearly three months, all the while feeding off each other's creativity. All we cared about was skating," Tony said. The film brought the genre of the skateboarding video to a whole new level, and parts of it were even shown on MTV.

The Search for Animal Chin sold well, and so did Tony's skateboards. Other companies, such as Stubbies Clothing and Tracker Trucks, took note of Tony's incredible style and massive popularity and offered him sponsorships. Soon he was making more than $200,000 a year.

Tony was winning contest after contest. He later said that the reason he won so often was because he always thought that his skating could improve, so he worked on it constantly. But there were still a few people who mocked Tony's skateboarding style. Not only that, Tony won so often that people seemed to expect him to come in first place all the time. When he didn't, they acted like he had lost. Instead of feeling pressure to do his best, Tony felt pressured to win all the time. And suddenly skateboarding didn't seem like much fun anymore.

So, at the age of nineteen Tony made a radical decision—he decided to retire from competition. He still wanted to skate, just not in contests. "The best thing is skating at home with a few friends and trying new stuff. I don't like competition that much," Tony later told reporters. So he took home his fifth NSA world championship award and said good-bye to competitive skateboarding.

But even though Tony wasn't in competitions anymore, he was still busy. He had started dating Cindy, and they were getting pretty serious. Tony also got small parts in a couple of movies, *Police Academy 4: Citizens on Patrol* and *Gleaming the Cube.* Tony bought a new house in Fallbrook. The house rested on four acres of land, and Tony's father helped him build an elaborate ramp and bowl in the backyard. Tony and Cindy moved into the house at the beginning of 1988, and Tony took time to relax and have fun while still working on his skating. But after three months of Tony's new life, he realized that something was missing—and that something was competitive skateboarding. He decided that he had to go back to it.

When Tony returned to competition, he found that he still had what it took to win. He took second in a contest in Irvine and then placed first in a competition in Toronto. Soon after, Tony appeared in the Bones Brigade's next video, *Public Domain*. Skating was peaking, and the video sold like crazy. The NSA started sponsoring competitions all over the world, and the prize money soared, sometimes reaching $10,000 for first place. "That was a great time for us," Tony said later. "We were making a ton of money and we flew all over the world." Even though Tony had taken off three months to explore other things, he still managed to make $100,000 that year. And the time off had cleared his mind—now he was more dedicated to skating than ever.

Chapter | Six

Hard Times

In the mid-1980s, street skating was just coming into its own. Skaters who didn't live near skateparks were looking for places to try out vert tricks, and the place they found was the street, which was lined with obstacles. A skater named Mark Gonzales was the first to take the ollie from the flat ground to a handrail. Skateboarders were amazed by this trick, and soon everyone wanted to do it. By 1989 street skating had taken off, and a whole new breed of skater was born.

Tony Hawk skated street style sometimes, but it wasn't as natural for him as vert skating was. That was a problem in 1989 because street skating's popularity was on the rise and vert's popularity was falling off. For one thing, anyone could skate street anywhere—you didn't have to go to a skatepark to practice—and some of the stunts were truly amazing. Street was popular not only because of the dangerous stunts it involved, but also because of its image. If vert skating was seen as a "rebel" sport, street skating was that times ten. For one thing, many street skaters actually practiced in the streets, which was against the law. Vert skating was sponsored by several large skateboarding companies, like Powell and Peralta, and Vision. But in the late eighties several smaller companies like World Industries and H-Street began to cater to the outlaw image that street skating fostered. Suddenly skate contests didn't really matter that much anymore because they didn't help sell skateboards. People were more interested in seeing street stunts. And the more dangerous they were, the better.

For many years skating's popularity seemed to go in nine-year cycles. It was up in the early 1970s, down by the end of the decade, up in the mid-1980s, and down in the early 1990s.

Soon riders began leaving the Bones Brigade. Their brand of skateboarding simply wasn't cool anymore, and Tony began to worry. He'd always loved the camaraderie of skateboarding. Not only did he get support from the Bones Brigade, Tony had always been friendly with skaters on other teams as well. But the new ideal skater image was that of a tough loner, and skateboarding as a whole began to take on a negative attitude. Skaters grew more competitive with one another. And since Tony was the number one skater, it seemed that everyone wanted to claw him from the top of the ranks. He was in his early twenties, and a lot of skaters considered him part of the "old school." They expected him to step aside and make way for the new, hot young skaters. Tony was so down on skating that he considered retiring . . . again. "I had done it so long and had reached the level I wanted to reach. It just wasn't fun anymore," he later told reporters.

To make matters worse, Tony injured himself while skating a demo in Japan. He was in so much pain that when he went to the airport to return to the United States, he had to use a wheel-chair to get to the plane. When he got home, a doctor told Tony that he would need to have surgery on his knee. It was the first time Tony had ever needed surgery, and he was pretty stressed out about it. He knew that he would have to stop skateboarding for almost four months. Even when he had retired from compe-tition, Tony had never taken time off from skateboarding.

Before the surgery, Tony agreed to skate a miniramp contest in Hawaii. Tony didn't want to miss the contest because it was his father's last one as head of the NSA. Frank Hawk's health wasn't good, and Nancy had managed to convince him to let someone else run the organization. Tony's knee was in bad shape, but he still managed to skate into fourth place and watch his father receive an award for his service to the NSA.

Tony has received over a dozen tickets for skateboarding!

Tony's knee surgery wasn't major—he didn't even have to stay in the hospital overnight. And luckily Tony was injured during a period when there weren't any vert contests, anyway. By the time his knee was healed, he was ready to jump right back into competitions.

In his first contest back, Tony took second place and then went on to win both the vert and street contests at the next competition, held in Denmark. Tony skated harder than ever and racked up win after win. He won vert contests and a couple of street contests as well. At the end of the year he was the NSA world champion once again. Powell released another video, *Ban This.* The video did well, and Tony made a lot of money that year—$150,000—but he was uncomfortable with the way things were changing in the world of skateboarding. He had no idea that they were about to get much worse.

Tony had been earning a lot of money, and he'd definitely been spending it instead of saving it. He was paying mortgages on two houses—the one in Fallbrook and the one in Carlsbad—and he constantly treated himself to expensive trips and electronic gadgets. He was acting like he expected skateboarding's popularity to last forever.

One day in early 1990 Tony and Cindy went shopping in Los Angeles and bought a diamond ring. They had talked a few times about getting married, and now they were engaged. They were married shortly afterward in a small ceremony in the backyard of the Fallbrook house and started to plan their future together.

Unfortunately, in the middle of the year skating's popularity just curled up and died. Tony's salary dried up, and so did contests and demos as the skateboarding companies began to trim their expenses. Even the NSA—suddenly unable to find sponsorship and now functioning without Frank Hawk's leadership and dedication—began to falter. It was like a flashback to the early days of Tony's career. The industry had little money, and the fans were disappearing. Tony went to a demo in Japan where the "crowd" consisted of fewer than thirty people. Just a couple of years earlier Tony would have expected the crowd to number in the thousands. At the end of the year, even though Tony picked up yet another NSA world champion trophy, his salary was half of what he had earned the year before.

In 1991 things got much worse. Tony was still winning contests and skating hard, but by the middle of the year he was earning less money than Cindy was making as a manicurist. They rented out the house in Carlsbad and put themselves on a budget. Tony even traded in his Lexus for a Honda Civic, but it was still hard to make ends meet.

The company he skated for, Powell and Peralta, was floundering, too. They tried to cut costs by rearranging the way they paid their skaters—that is, by paying them less—but there was nothing that they could do about the fact that people simply weren't interested in skating anymore. Also, Powell and Peralta had been trying to change its clean-cut image to match the new tough, in-your-face style that street skating had brought into vogue. But the strategy blew up in Powell's face. Skaters didn't buy their sudden change in attitude, and their attempt to follow the smaller companies' lead only gave the little guys more cred. "Throughout the nineties, we were given a bad rap because we had been a really large company in the eighties," George Powell later said. "It wasn't cool to be a big company." Powell and Peralta was in financial trouble, and it didn't look like things were going to get better anytime soon.

That was when Tony decided that it was time for a change. But he didn't have a college degree, and he didn't know how to do anything but skateboard. So, even though he knew that he had to do something different, the question was—what?

❝*I never set a plan for my life, I just rolled with it.*❞
—TONY HAWK

Chapter Seven

Welcome to the Birdhouse

By the time Tony was almost twenty-four, he had been skating professionally for almost ten years, and he was tired of being just another sponsored skateboarder on the team. He saw what was going wrong with Powell, and he wanted to have more say in the decision making, so he teamed up with another former member of the Bones Brigade, Per Welinder, to form a company.

Per was a freestyler who had retired from contest skating in 1989 to pursue a degree in marketing. Once he graduated from Long Beach State University, Per went to work for Powell, managing new products. Per and Tony planned their new business in secret for months. They named the company Birdhouse—a reference to Tony's nickname, "Birdman"—and calculated that they would need $100,000 to get things started. Tony had to take out a second mortgage on his house in Carlsbad to contribute his share. Not many people would have put all of their money into a skateboarding company just when it appeared that skating had disappeared from the radar screen, but then again, Tony was never "most people." He had risen to the top of the skateboarding profession by taking extreme risks, and starting a company—in his mind—was a lot safer than some of the tricks he tried on his skateboard. In January 1992 Birdhouse was officially formed.

A few weeks after Tony announced his plan to leave the Bones Brigade to George Powell and Stacy Peralta, Peralta called Tony with his own piece of news—he wanted to be a director. Tony and his mentor were leaving Powell at the same time to pursue their separate dreams.

Tony was happy with his decision to start Birdhouse. He had already recruited an incredibly talented group of skateboarders to ride for the company—Steve Berra, Ocean Howell, Jeremy Klein, Mike Frazier, and Willy Santos—and he felt confident that the company would take off. But Birdhouse was slow to get off the ground. No matter how talented the skate team was and how good their product, skateboarding had disappeared from the national scene. Part of the problem was that other new "action" sports were becoming more popular, including the all-new sport of in-line skating. Skateboarding was losing ground fast.

But that was okay with Tony. In Tony's autobiography, he says that he loved the lean years because he knew that anyone who was still skating was doing it for the love of the sport. That was definitely what Tony was doing. Most of his sponsorships had disappeared, and Birdhouse was hardly paying him anything at all. And he wasn't the only one who was hurting—Steve Berra had to move into Tony's house in Fallbrook in order to save money.

The year he started Birdhouse, Tony's life changed in another major way—he found out that he was going to be a father. Babies cost money, and now Tony and Cindy had to pinch every penny that came their way. Tony put himself on a tight budget—Cindy only gave him five dollars a day. But Tony took it in stride and jokingly referred to this as his "Taco Bell allowance" since that was where most of his money went.

In the spring of 1992 Birdhouse released their first two pro skateboards—one Jeremy Klein model and one Willy Santos. That's right—at first there was no Birdhouse Tony Hawk skateboard. "We did not release a Tony Hawk board since vert skating had become much less popular compared to street," Tony's Birdhouse partner, Per Welinder, later explained in an interview.

Between the years 1987 and 1993 the number of skate-boarders in the United States dropped by half.

That summer Tony and Per decided to put their skate-boarding team on a demo tour. Tony knew that he had to be visible within the skateboarding community if his name was going to continue to carry any weight and sell skateboards. It was a strictly low-budget affair, with the guys sleeping five to a room in cheap motels. But there was a problem—even though stores were supposed to pay the Birdhouse team for their demos, often they simply refused to fork over the cash (which was never that much to begin with). Even though Tony had tried to do the tour on as little money as possible, there was no way to fight the fact that the fans and the money just weren't there.

Still, wherever Tony went, he was always friendly to the fans, taking the time to chat with them and sign autographs. He knew that if skateboarding was going to come back, it would be because of grassroots support. Despite Tony's and the team's best efforts, by the end of the summer Birdhouse had lost over $7,000 on the tour. The crew was still hopeful that the money would start to flow once word got out about how tight their skate team was. Unfortunately, it was taking a while for people to notice.

By the end of the year Tony began to worry about the future of skateboarding and Birdhouse's moneymaking prospects. He decided that he needed to try to make money some other way and borrowed $8,000 from his parents to buy some video-editing equipment. He edited videos for several skateboard companies and even worked on a series of instructional surfing videos. But it turned out that editing wasn't the path to riches, either, and eventually Tony decided to focus his energy on making Birdhouse a success.

Tony's son Riley was born on December 6, 1992. Tony's skateboarding buddies loved his baby immediately and lavished attention on him. Even though money was tight, Tony enjoyed fatherhood. Still, he had to come to terms with his financial situation, which was only getting worse. The ramps in his backyard were showing signs of wear and Tony didn't have the money to fix them. Eventually he was forced to sell the house in Fallbrook and move back into his smaller, more affordable house in Carlsbad, California.

Riley's real name is Hudson Riley Hawk. But the year he was born, a movie starring Bruce Willis was released and bombed. The name of the movie? *Hudson Hawk*. For this and other reasons, Tony decided to call his son by his middle name.

Tony's senior yearbook photo

Working the ramp at the
1997 ESPN X Games

Performing in the vert
competition at the
X Games in 1998

Andy Macdonald and Tony (right) take to the air at the 2000 X Games.

Tony poses with his award for Best Video Game—*Tony Hawk's Pro Skater 2*—at the 2001 Blockbuster Awards.

Hamming it up after winning his Teen Choice Award in 2001

Tony hangs with Tom Green at the 2002 ESPN Action Sports and Music Awards.

Leaping into the air during a demonstration of *Tony Hawk's Pro Skater 3* video game at the eighth annual 2002 Electronic Entertainment Expo in Los Angeles, California.

The Hawk family—Tony, wife Erin, and sons Keegan, Spencer, and Riley—at the premiere of *Stuart Little 2*.

Tony takes to the air at the SkyDome in Toronto, Canada, in 2002.

That summer Tony went back on tour with Birdhouse. This time Birdhouse lost $6,000—$1,000 less than the year before. By the end of the year Tony had basically stopped competing. Vert was dying, and Tony felt lucky if he counted more than fifteen people in the stands at contests. If he did win prize money, the checks would often bounce. Finally Tony decided to retire again. He wanted to focus on the business aspect of his company and leave the skating to the rest of the talented guys on his team.

As though the challenges with his business weren't enough, in 1994 things began to unravel for Tony on a personal level as well—he and Cindy were legally separated. Tony and Cindy were never bitter toward each other; they just realized that they couldn't live together anymore. They agreed to joint custody of Riley—Tony took care of him from Monday to Friday, while Cindy watched him over the weekends—and devoted themselves to making sure that he was cared for. Within a few months they decided to divorce.

But through it all, Tony never stopped taking care of Birdhouse. He still had faith that the company would eventually show a profit.

❝I never imagined a future for myself outside skateboarding.❞

—TONY HAWK

Chapter Eight

Extreme Scene

Even though Tony wasn't entering skating competitions anymore, he was still practicing every day. Since he no longer had a ramp in his backyard, he skated at the local YMCA. He was learning and inventing new tricks, and his skating was getting better and better. At around the same time a new word entered the vocabulary of sports—*extreme.* Cable television had brought action sports to a wider audience, and a minor teen population boom—the children of the baby boomers—was fascinated with these sports' raw energy. Suddenly people were interested in watching thrilling, dangerous-looking sports, one of which was skateboarding. Skateboarding faced another happy change as well—new laws lowered the cost of insurance for skateparks, and people began building them again. All of a sudden Tony and his team were in demand to perform demos, which they happily did. It still didn't pay much, but the crowds were growing, and that was enough for Tony.

In the spring of 1995 Tony was asked to perform in a brand-new show called *Extreme Wheels Live!* The show was being put together by Jill Schulz, who is the daughter of *Peanuts* creator Charles M. Schulz. Jill Schulz's plan was for a performance of not only skateboarding, but in-line skating and BMX biking as well. It was to be an exciting show, but one that didn't focus on the outsider, rebel aspects of extreme sports. Instead *Extreme Wheels Live!* was to be a show that the whole family could watch together.

One of the in-line skaters performing in the show was a University of San Diego student named Erin. Erin and Tony hit it off right away, and Erin was crazy about Tony's son, Riley, who took after his father. Riley could already do an ollie at the age of three! Tony spent whatever time he could hanging out with his son, teaching him not only skateboarding, but baseball and basketball as well, just as his own father had done for him. Soon Erin was spending a lot of time with Riley and Tony.

After a few months of retirement Tony once again had to accept the fact that he missed competing. In addition, Birdhouse still wasn't out of financial trouble. Tony knew that if he competed in a few events and did well, the publicity would be good for the company. So Tony and Per came up with a new Tony Hawk skateboard, and Tony went back to what he did best. His timing was impeccable.

In 1995 a cable channel known as the Entertainment Sports Network, or ESPN, decided to create and air a new event for extreme sports. ESPN broadcasts sports twenty-four hours a day, and they don't limit their events to football, basketball, and baseball. Instead they broadcast all sorts of events, including the newer action sports. Their new event idea was intended to appeal to a young audience and would be modeled on the Olympics, but it would be for sports like street luge, in-line skating, and— you guessed it—skateboarding. The name of the event was the Extreme Games, which later morphed to the shorter (and cooler-sounding) X Games.

Not all skateboarders were excited about the idea of the Extreme Games. Many skaters worried that ESPN would portray

Never underestimate the power of television.

—TONY HAWK

them as reckless rebels and that their sport would suffer even more. Others were worried that the sport would appear too mainstream and would alienate the people who preferred its outsider status. As far back as 1986 Kevin Thatcher, then editor of *Thrasher* magazine, told *Sports Illustrated,* "We don't want to see skateboarding in the Olympics." And now here was an Olympics-style event ready to showcase this "rebel" sport!

Tony had mixed feelings, but the Extreme Games were offering something that he simply couldn't resist—a vert contest. Many competitions had eliminated vert entirely, preferring to focus on the more popular street courses. Tony knew that the Extreme Games were a golden opportunity for him to shine in his strongest event. It would also be a golden opportunity to introduce skateboarding to a mass audience.

> What do Madonna and Saran Wrap have in common?
> They're both skateboarding tricks invented by Tony Hawk!

In June 1995 the first Extreme Games were held in Newport, Rhode Island. Tony entered both the vert and street contests. The Extreme Games were a huge success for ESPN. Almost 200,000 fans showed up to see the events live, and millions of people around the world tuned in to watch Tony take

> 66*Without a doubt, Tony Hawk is one of the greatest in the sport. He can get his body to do what his brain sees.*99
> —MARK WHITELEY, EDITOR OF *SLAP*

first place in vert and second in street. Suddenly his popularity took off! For the first time in his life Tony was an athlete whom people recognized wherever he went.

Another exciting thing happened as a result of ESPN's skateboarding competition broadcast—people became totally pumped about vert skating! The fact was, vert tricks looked amazing on TV, and Tony was the one doing the sickest skating. His first place win helped to bring about a vert revival.

But 1995 didn't bring only good news for Tony. In the spring of that year, just before the Extreme Games, Frank Hawk was diagnosed with cancer. Tony was very concerned about his father and offered to stay with him while he underwent chemotherapy. But Frank Hawk wouldn't hear of it. He knew that Tony had to look after Riley, and he understood that Tony's career was important to him. Frank had always been Tony's biggest supporter when it came to skateboarding, and he didn't want his son to give up on it now. Frank wasn't able to go to Rhode Island to watch Tony place in the X Games finals, but he did watch his son on television. It must have meant a great deal to Frank to know that millions of people were watching his son compete in a sport that he himself had done so much to progress.

Summer is skateboarding's busiest season, and Tony was supposed to go on tour with the Birdhouse team again, but he canceled to spend more time with his father. Then he quickly had to *un*cancel when his father insisted—in his special military style—that Tony go on the tour. Still, Tony was worried about his father and phoned him every night while he was away. It turned out that his fears were well-founded. One night, while Tony was still on the road, Frank died peacefully in his sleep. Tony flew home right away for his father's wake. A few hundred people were there, many of whom were skateboarders who had come to express their sadness and gratitude for everything that Frank had done for them and for the sport of skateboarding.

Tony knew that his father wouldn't have wanted him to stop skateboarding, so he kept right on competing—and winning. That year Airwalk came out with a Tony Hawk shoe. Thanks to publicity from the X Games, Birdhouse's sales improved dramatically, and suddenly Tony was making money again. It wasn't a lot, but it was enough so that he could stop worrying a little. Skateboarding was definitely making a comeback. And so was Tony.

Tony decided that he needed more time to practice skating, so he commissioned a private ramp in a warehouse in Irvine. Now that skating's popularity had taken off again, Tony was busier than ever, practicing hard and traveling to compete and perform demos. Someone had to take care of Riley, so Erin volunteered to help. Tony and Erin had become very close, and Erin seemed to fit naturally into Tony's family. Soon Tony asked her to marry him. She said yes, and the wedding took place on September 28, 1996.

In 1996 Tony twisted his ankle severely while skating in the X Games qualifying event, Destination Extreme. He tried to ignore the injury and toured with the Birdhouse team, but eventually the pain caught up with him, and he had to stop skating for a while. Tony was starting to worry that perhaps he was getting too old for his sport. But after a month he felt that he had recovered enough to skate in the X Games, which were once again to be held in Rhode Island. Tony skated well, but not as well as he had the year before—he came in second in vert and

In twenty years of skateboarding, Tony never broke a single bone . . . until he fell from his skateboard and shattered his elbow while filming an ad for the Gap!

seventh in street. But it wasn't bad for someone who had just come back from an injury. Tony was stoked—he had done well enough to convince himself that he still had what it took to skate competitively.

"*I don't think about my age when I skate.***"**

—TONY HAWK

By 1997 skateboarding had launched from the rocket pad yet again. Birdhouse sales were exceeding all expectations, selling thousands of decks a month. They even added a clothing line—Hawk Clothing. Tony wasn't just skating demos and contests anymore. He was being asked to skate in commercials for companies like Schick. Suddenly Tony's schedule was booked solid, and he asked his sister Pat, who had a background in entertainment, to help out as his manager. Pat persuaded a friend to act as Tony's publicist, and soon Tony was doing cool magazine interviews to promote his company and the sport of skateboarding.

That year Tony had an incredible X Games. He had decided not to compete in the street contest and instead focus all of his energy on his number one sport—vert. In the X Games skaters perform three forty-five-second runs, in which skaters are judged on the technical difficulty of their tricks and on their style and execution. The winner is the skater who gets the highest score on any single run. The announcers called Tony's second run during the vert event "perfect," and he skated into first place. Even better, Tony competed in the brand-new vert doubles event with his friend Andy Macdonald, who had won the vert event the year before and was Tony's main competition. Most skaters don't compete in doubles because it is difficult and can be dangerous. If one of the competitors is off by even a fraction of a second, both skaters risk slamming and injury. But Tony and Andy skated perfectly, and they won the vert doubles contest—together!

By 1998 Birdhouse was going strong, and Tony felt that it was time to really showcase his team. He decided to do what his old team, the Bones Brigade, had done to boost their popularity—produce a video. But Tony didn't want to produce a video that looked like the ones that the other companies already had on the market, most of which were poorly done. He wanted to produce something that would match—and even surpass—the

Before she became his manager, Tony's sister Pat used to sing backup for Michael Bolton!

best of the Powell and Peralta videos. Tony let his skaters come up with their own stunts and sketches. He gave everyone on the team a budget to spend as they liked. The result was *The End*, a raucous skate video featuring daring stunts, some of which were performed by skaters in flaming suits. Naturally, the video was an enormous success.

With everything in his skating life going so well, Tony had to wonder what he would do to top himself next.

Chapter | Nine

900

fter Tony's "perfect" run at the 1997 X Games, he spent his entire third run trying to complete a 900. Skateboarding events are judged by a skateboarder's best run. Since Tony had already had a good one, he knew that he didn't have to worry— he could attempt 900s to his heart's content. But he didn't land one that day. In fact, he got nowhere close.

The 900 was a trick that Tony had wanted to pull for years. In his career Tony has invented close to a hundred tricks, but the one he cared most about was a grueling two-and-a-half-spin midair rotation. (The 900 gets its name from the degrees of a circle. One full circle is 360 degrees, two full circles is 720, and two and a half is 900.)

Tony had first learned to land a 720 in 1985, when he was working at a skateboarding camp in Sweden. For a long time, however, Tony landed every 720 in an ugly, wobbly squat. But

Once Tony spent five minutes trying to land a 900, only to end up having to go to the doctor's office twice that day.

after a couple of years he had truly mastered them, and he often landed one to complete his competition runs. Still, Tony wasn't satisfied with only two rotations. He felt that he could take the trick further.

Tony had been trying the 900 off and on since 1986, but he really began to get serious in 1996 and began attempting one almost every time he skated on a vert ramp. He actually did land one that year—but immediately toppled off his deck and fell face first onto the bottom of the ramp, fracturing a rib.

According to his autobiography, when Tony shot his segment for the Birdhouse video, *The End,* he planned to perform the three tricks he had always wanted to pull—a varial 720 (in which a skater goes up the ramp backward, spins twice, turns the board around beneath his feet, and skates back down the ramp backward), a clean loop, and a 900. For the shoot Tony had a humongous custom ramp with a loop at the end built in a bullring in Tijuana, Mexico. Tony skated the ramp for six days but didn't even try a 900 until the last day. That's because a skater can get seriously injured doing a 900, and Tony didn't want to get hurt before the director got some footage of him skating. Tony landed the varial 720 fairly easily, then went to work trying to skate a clean loop. Unfortunately, a full loop is an incredibly difficult thing to skate. Tony fell often before landing one cleanly, and as a result, he wasn't able to attempt the 900. He was upset and disappointed with himself, but there wasn't much that he could do about it, except try again another time.

Tony did keep trying . . . and he kept slamming. Needless to say, falling while trying to perform such a trick is very hard on the body. As Tony later told a reporter, "You can only spin 900s for so long before you're just wrecked. Even if you're landing safely, the impact gets to you." It looked like the 900 was the one trick that would elude Tony forever.

❝I just figured I was either going to land it, or I was going to wake up later in the hospital.**❞**

—TONY HAWK, ON THE 900

Early in 1999 Tony decided that this really would be his last year of competition. Tony had been skating competitively for twenty years and attempting the 900 for thirteen without ever landing one. It looked like he would end his career without that trick on his list of accomplishments.

❝I don't plan on trying a 1080.**❞**

—TONY HAWK,
ON WHAT'S NEXT FOR HIS CAREER

But Tony was content—his career was still going well, and he was booked with loads of endorsement deals and commercials. Plus his second son, Spencer, was born on March 26, 1999. Things were going well for Tony all around, and he figured that he could live without "The Trick."

When Tony went to the 1999 X Games, he knew that it would be his last time skating in the event. Unfortunately, he didn't perform as well as he had hoped in the vert contest and only took third place. First place went to his friend Bucky Lasek.

But the vert contest wasn't the only event that Tony was scheduled to skate in that year. He was also signed up for the Best Trick contest.

The Best Trick event is scored in a similar way to the vert event—whoever pulls the best single trick in half an hour of skating wins. It doesn't matter if you slam on fifty tricks and only land one good one. If your one trick is better than anyone else's, you win. Tony hoped that he could win the event with a varial 720 and landed one early in the event. Since that was his best trick and he had already landed it cleanly, Tony decided to spend the rest of his time trying for a 900. After all, if he fell, it wouldn't affect his chances of winning. And, as Tony later noted, after the 720, "the only place to go was the 900."

Tony tried a few 900s. Even though he wasn't nailing them, he knew that he was getting closer—he almost had it. Then the announcers said that the time was up. But Tony didn't stop skating. He knew that he could land the trick if he kept trying. He didn't care about the event; he just wanted to hit that 900. It was like the moment, years before, when his father had called to him, trying to get him to stop skating and come home for supper. Tony just couldn't stop skating. Even if it took another five hundred tries, he just had to get it.

❝*I feel like if I'm not out there getting banged up, then I'm not getting better.*❞

—TONY HAWK

Tony tried the trick ten times, and all ten, he slammed. But by then everyone knew what he was trying to do. The fans were behind him. The other skaters in the event—Bucky Lasek, Colin McKay, Bob Burnquist, and Andy Macdonald—were behind him. Everyone wanted Tony to land the trick, even though the event was supposed to be over already! After a while the announcer said, "This is the X Games. We make up the rules as we go along. Let's give him another try!"

Tony rolled to the top of the half pipe twice, gaining velocity. Then he took to the air, held his board with his right hand and spun his body two and a half times, and landed on his board. He looked a bit awkward at first, and the spectators held their breath, wondering if he would fall. But he straightened up as he rolled across the flat bottom of the ramp, and there was no doubt about it—he had landed the trick. Tony looked stunned, but the crowd knew what to do—they went wild! His skateboarding friends hauled him up onto their shoulders, laughing and cheering. Tony told everyone that it was "the best day of his life." Which it definitely was, as far as his skating career was concerned. Hawk had just landed a trick that would go down in skateboarding history.

Tony finished out the year of competition, appearing in the Vans Triple Crowns finals and the MTV Best Trick and Highest Air events. He landed another 900 in the MTV event and was finally ready to retire from competition. And this time, it would be for good.

❝That's the only time I've seen him run.❞

—GRANT BRITTAIN,
ON TONY HAWK CARRYING THE OLYMPIC TORCH

Even though Tony left his competitive life behind, his sudden fame ensured that his name would always be associated with skateboarding excellence. As an acknowledgment of Tony's important role in the history and development of skateboarding, on January 14, 2002, Tony was given the honor of carrying the Olympic torch in San Diego.

Tony was allowed to keep the Olympic torch—for $250.

Chapter | Ten

Citizen Hawk

Retirement had never changed much about Tony's life before, and it certainly didn't this time. But he has chosen to spend more quality time with his family. Tony and Erin had a third son, Keegan, on July 18, 2001, and Tony often has his hands full helping out around the house and taking care of his sons. He even gets up early every morning to make breakfast for the family.

But don't think that Tony has lost his love of skating. He still skates all the time and travels to perform demos. He's simply made his family his number one priority. "I just try to include my family as much as I can," Tony said in a recent interview. "I try to take my son [Riley] with me, and if it's not too much of a strain, I take everyone." Tony also remains committed to promoting skateboarding and has managed to bring it to the mainstream world in many different ways.

If you aren't interested in skating, you've probably still heard the name Tony Hawk because of his video game, *Tony Hawk's Pro Skater,* which is produced by Activision. Tony and Activision came together to work on the game in 1998. Not only did Tony test the game, he even skated for some of the motion-capture sessions. That means he wore a suit covered with sensors while he skated, and special cameras captured his movements so that the programmers could use them in the game.

Tony thought that the game was cool, and he thought that people would like it, but he wasn't prepared for the wild success that followed almost immediately after the video game's release. Not only did skaters love the game for its cool, realistic skate moves, even mainstream people with little interest in or knowledge of skating appreciated it. *Tony Hawk's Pro Skater* came out in the fall of 1999, and by the Christmas season it was the top-selling video game. In 2001 *Pro Skater* was the number two best-selling sports video game for the year. The game has been through three versions—*Pro Skater 4* was released in November 2002—and is still selling strong.

In fall 2002 Tony appeared as a guest voice on *The Simpsons.* He played himself and dueled with Homer on the vert ramp!

> **❝**If I had truly sold out, I'd just be living off royalties and I'd never get on another skateboard.**❞**
>
> —Tony Hawk

Also, Tony probably appears on television more now than he ever did before. In 1999 Tony put together *Tony Hawk's Gigantic Skatepark Tour,* a show for ESPN, which showcased not only skate competitions, but what the skaters and their lives were like. The show was an enormous hit and garnered huge ratings, and Tony went on to do another *Skatepark Tour* in 2001 and again in 2002. His son Riley even came along for the latest tour. Not only that, Tony signed a three-year contract as a skateboarding commentator for ESPN. Tony has also appeared on the MTV show *Jackass.* Once he dressed up as a chicken and skateboarded into a lake. For the *Jackass* movie, Tony rolled around on a half pipe dressed up in a fat suit.

Tony is the master of many media. His autobiography, coauthored with Sean Mortimer, was published by HarperCollins in 2000 and quickly climbed onto the *New York Times* bestseller list. And in 2001 Tony appeared in the documentary movie *Dogtown and Z-Boys*, which is about the influential Zephyr skateboarding team. The director of the movie was none other than Tony's Bones Brigade mentor, Stacy Peralta.

Now that his professional skateboarding days are over, Tony has more endorsement deals than ever, and his business is booming. Birdhouse and Blitz Distribution (another skateboard company that Tony and Per Welinder own) do nearly $25 million worth of sales a year. Tony's clothing line, which he started in 1998 and eventually sold to Quiksilver, brings in about $13 million in revenue a year. Tony Hawk Inc. is a business that employs seventy-five people. His *Pro Skater* video game has an average sale of $180 million every year. Tony endorses Heinz's Bagel Bites, sales of which have risen twenty percent since he signed on. In fact, when Tony appeared at a Bagel Bites booth at the 2000 Winter X Games, the crowd that gathered to see him was so large that Heinz was forced to get extra security. Mattel makes a Tony Hawk brand remote-controlled skateboard and Hot Wheels figure. And Tony even owns a production company, 900 Films, which produced the *Gigantic Skatepark Tour* and the WB's show *What I Like About You* (he appeared in the premiere episode as himself).

Altogether, products bearing Tony Hawk's name have combined sales of more than $250 million every year. Not bad for a guy who, growing up, never thought that he'd be able to make any money from skateboarding.

But Tony isn't all about making money on sponsorship deals. He also started the Tony Hawk Foundation, a fund to help build public skateparks in underprivileged areas. The executive director of the fund is Tony's brother, Steve Hawk. So far, the fund has helped create sixty-five skateparks across the country. This year the Tony Hawk Foundation is expected to distribute almost half a million dollars in grants. "We give out one or two $25,000 grants, two or three $10,000 grants, and the rest will be $5,000 and $1,000 grants," Steve explained. "We do that four times a year."

The Tony Hawk Foundation is run differently from most nonprofits, which tend to invest most of their income. The nonprofits then give away only the money they earn on their investments but don't touch the original money. That way they can continue to give away money for a long time in the future. But the Tony Hawk Foundation has a different plan. "We've decided to spend about 80 percent of our annual income every year, because hundreds of skateparks are going to be built or designed over the next couple of years, and we need to help these people now," Steve said.

In fact, the Tony Hawk Foundation has been flooded with applications since it was first founded. But don't think that they'll give you money to build a sick ramp in your backyard— the Tony Hawk Foundation only gives money to public charities, state or local agencies (like public schools), and start-up organizations. Also, the park being built has to meet certain rules to get the money. For example, the park can't charge money, and the foundation prefers to fund parks that will be open 365 days a year.

Tony donates all of his demo fees to the foundation, which also receives a percentage of sales of Hawk Clothing and has been given gifts, including $50,000 from Activision. In the fall of 2001 Tony even appeared on the celebrity athletes version of *Who Wants to Be a Millionaire* and won $125,000 for the Tony Hawk Foundation. Tony often promotes the foundation in interviews to be sure that it receives plenty of exposure.

It seems that in retirement, Tony Hawk has managed to do more to bring skateboarding to the world than he did when he was still competing!

❝_Tony Hawk means ka-ching._**❞**

—JAKE PHELPS,
LONGTIME EDITOR OF *THRASHER* MAGAZINE

Hawk Flies High

Tony Hawk's latest big project is the Boom Boom Huckjam tour. The name was his idea and is based on skate lingo. "Huck" means to get airborne, and a "jam" is like a musical jam, in which talented people get together and combine their talent for a cool show. "Boom Boom" just means a cool experience, which Tony really hoped the show would be.

Tony originally conceived of the Huckjam as an Ice Capades–style show in which skateboarders and freestyle BMX and motocross riders would perform tightly choreographed routines to live rock music. The idea for the show arose from Tony's desire both to deliver these "alternative" sports to a mass audience and to help prolong the careers of the riders. Competitive skateboarding, motocross, and BMX can be very dangerous, as riders perform increasingly challenging and difficult stunts to win. A choreographed show in which riders perform moves that they have perfected on a customized ramp reduces the risk of serious injury, at least in theory.

Tony was confident that this kind of show would still deliver thrills for mainstream audiences while allowing serious fans a glimpse at alternative athletes who rarely appear on TV. At first, Tony had a hard time raising sponsorship money for the show. But he really believed in it, so he put up over $1 million of his own money to make the first show happen. To perform, Tony recruited the top athletic talent in the field: Bob Burnquist, Bucky Lasek, and Andy Macdonald for skateboarding, Mat Hoffman and Dave Mirra for BMX, and Carey Hart, Mike Cinqmars, and Clifford Adopante for motocross, among others. "I chose the skaters . . . not necessarily for their competition records," Tony Hawk said in an interview, "but because I think each one represents a different style." For the live music, Tony signed up the alterna-rock bands Offspring and Social Distortion. Even though the event was conceived as a venue to showcase action sports, the bands were psyched to be involved. "I think the music just goes hand in hand with those kind of sports. I love it," Noodles, of Offspring, said before the show.

Still, even with this lineup of amazing talent, Tony was nervous before the show premiered. The truth was, not everything had gone smoothly in rehearsals. There had been a couple of near misses in which riders could have gotten really hurt, and there was one serious accident—motocross rider Drake McElroy overshot his first jump and fractured his jaw. After that, Tony was really worried. He and the show's creative director, Morgan Stone (who also directed Tony's *Gigantic Skatepark Tour*), knew that most of their athletes were used to performing solo. "The hardest part . . . has been the choreography, because a lot of these guys aren't used to . . . having to worry about other riders, and where they're going to have to be," Morgan Stone said.

But even with all of the risks, Tony had high hopes for the show. He knew that everything hinged on the premiere at Mandalay Bay Events Center in Las Vegas. If the riders could get the choreography down, the event would be unbelievable. "This first show is either going to be a huge success or the most expensive party I've ever thrown for a bunch of my friends," Tony told a reporter for *Sports Illustrated*.

Naturally, the show came off perfectly. It was a huge hit, and Tony immediately decided to go ahead with a full tour in the

---

❝*Here's what skateboarding is to me. It's my form of exercise, my sport, my means of expression since I was nine years old. It's what I love. I never expected it to give me anything more than that.*❞

—TONY HAWK

fall. He even managed to line up sponsors for the tour, including Activision 2 and PlayStation 2. The show kicked off on October 9 in Portland, performed in major stadium venues across the country, and wrapped up in Fort Lauderdale on November 17. The athletes varied throughout the run, as did the rock performers, who included such bands as Face to Face, Devo, and CKY in addition to Offspring and Social Distortion. By all accounts, Tony accomplished his goal with the show, which was, as he told *Sports Illustrated,* to "build something that will live beyond my involvement in it." Given its success, there is little doubt that the Huckjam will continue to perform for enthusiastic crowds for years to come.

66*Parents look at [Tony] and say, 'I don't mind my kid doing that. He's Mr. Straight Guy.'***99**

—STACY PERALTA

Tony's son Riley seems to take after his dad. "He's enjoyed playing soccer and basketball," Tony told a reporter in 1998, "but lately he's become attracted to the skatepark. Whenever I say I'm going there, he always wants to go with me." Riley is a talented skater who has appeared with his dad in a commercial for Disney's *Tarzan* and *Max Keeble's Big Move.* In the summer of 2002 he went along for Tony's *Gigantic Skateboard Tour.*

Even though Tony has said that he would encourage any of his sons to pursue a career in skateboarding if that was what they wanted, he has also said that he would want them to be realistic. He would want them to understand that a skateboarding career can end suddenly as a result of an injury, so it's important to have a good education.

66*If my role is to be skateboarding's link to the mainstream, I'm willing to accept it.*99

—TONY HAWK

Tony has a few other major plans in the works. His production company, 900 Films, is working on a biopic about his life. The Disney company purchased the film rights to Tony's autobiography, *Hawk: Occupation: Skateboarder,* and Tony will be the executive producer on the film. The movie will be released in 2003 and will chronicle Tony's life as he went from an awkward teenager to skateboarding hero. Tony will also continue to appear on television and in movies, playing himself. (He's said that he does not want to be an actor.)

As for the future of the Tony Hawk Foundation, Tony has big aspirations for his little fund. "I would like us to get to a point where we can fund entire parks," Tony said. "Right now, we can only help them get started." The foundation is partnering with the Los Angeles School District for a program called Beyond the Bell, in which eleven portable skateparks will be built—one for each of the school districts in LA. Kids will be allowed to skate there twice a week, with adults on hand to supervise. The Tony Hawk Foundation is also putting together a general information package with tips and suggestions for building skateparks. Parks and towns can use the information to create skateparks that are fun, challenging, and, most important, safe.

As Tony told a reporter, "I want to give something back to the skateboard community; it's been very good to me." Of course, many would say that Tony has already given the sport of skateboarding his all . . . and then some. And there's no doubt that he'll continue to give it more for a long time to come.

"Learn the basics, learn to fall, learn perseverance, and follow your heart.**"

—TONY HAWK,
ON HOW TO LEARN TO SKATEBOARD

GLOSSARY

Air: A trick in which a skater leaves the ground

Am: An amateur, a skater who is not a professional

Axle: The pin that holds the wheels in place

Bail: To fall off a skateboard during a trick

Bank: A sloped surface in which the incline is less than 90 degrees

Board: Sometimes called a "deck," this is the "board" part of the skateboard. It is most often made of maple laminate

Caballerial: Named for Steve Caballero, this is a trick in which a skater skates to the top of the coping and does a complete turn in the air without grabbing his board, then skates back down into the bowl.

Carve: 1. To ride in a long curving arc, with all four wheels touching the ground 2. In vert, when one goes airborne, to carve means to soar through the air in a half circle.

Compressing: To crouch or bend while on a skateboard in order to gain momentum and/or balance easily

Coping: The rounded edge at the lip of a pool or ramp, usually made of metal, cement, or pipe

Drop in: To skate into a bowl or half pipe from the top

Early-grab: To grab your board before you catch air

Fakie: Initiating a trick with your forward foot

Flatbottom: The flat surface at the base of a transition

Freestyle: An old-school form of skateboarding in which competitors perform smooth, graceful tricks and carves on a flat surface, usually performed to music

Frontside: When a skater approaches an obstacle or a trick with the nose end of his board pointing forward

Goofy-foot: Riding a skateboard with your right foot positioned near the nose of the board and your rear foot near the tail

Grab: To hold the board with your hand while performing a trick in the air

Grind: A trick in which a skater rides up to an obstacle and scrapes his axles against the edge

Half pipe: A skating ramp in the shape of a U or semicircle, which resembles a piece of pipe that has been sawed in half lengthwise

Handrail: A rail on a set of stairs, often used as an obstacle in street skating

Invert: A trick in which the skater skates up to the coping, places one hand on the surface and does a handstand while holding on to his deck with the other hand, then skates back into the bowl

Kickflip: A trick in which the skater uses his toe to turn the board over in a complete flip and lands back on the board, which is facing right-side up

Kicktail: The tail of the board, which is angled upward to enable skaters to turn and jump

Kickturn: A trick in which a skater presses down on the tail of his deck in order to lift the front wheels off the ground, then uses momentum to turn the board in another direction

Launch: When a skater is soaring through the air

Lip: The top edge of a half pipe or pool

Madonna: A trick invented by Tony Hawk, which was named after the singer because it "takes your breath away"

Nose: The front end of a skateboard

Nosegrind: A move in which only the front axles grind against an obstacle

Noseslide: A trick in which the skater slides the nose of the board against an obstacle, coping, curb, or lip

Ollie: A trick that makes a skater airborne without holding his board. Invented by Alan Gelfand, this is the basis of most tricks.

Quarter pipe: A ramp that forms one-half of a U

Rad: Cool or good—derived from the word *radical*

Rail: 1. The outer edge of the skateboard 2. A plastic strip that runs lengthwise along the underside of a skateboard and eases sliding or grabbing

Railslide: To slide on a surface (like a curb, rail, or coping) in a position so that the rail is the only part of the skateboard to come into contact with the obstacle

Rip: Skate superwell

Shred: Skate superwell

Sick: Excellent

Slam: A harsh, unexpected fall, usually one in which the skater is hurt or injured

Stoked: Excited, happy

Street: A form of skating in which skaters use benches, curbs, stair rails, and other pieces of urban street furniture to perform their tricks

Tail: The rear end of a skate deck

Thrasher: A skateboarder

Transition: A riding surface that is on an incline, like the curved part of a ramp or half pipe

Truck: The part of the skateboard that fastens the axles and wheels to the skate decks and allows the board to turn

Vert: Or vertical, a form of skateboarding in which skaters perform tricks on a half pipe

Vert ramp: A half pipe in which the steepest part of the U is almost completely vertical

STATS

Full name:
Anthony Frank Hawk

Birthplace:
San Diego, California

Birth date:
May 12, 1968

Height:
6' 3"

Weight:
170

Marital status:
Married

Children:
3

Number of skateboarding world championships:
12

Number of tricks invented:
80+

X GAMES HISTORY

SUMMER 2001	VERT BEST TRICK	2
SUMMER 2001	VERT DOUBLES	1
SUMMER 2000	VERT DOUBLES	1
SUMMER 1999	VERT	3
SUMMER 1999	VERT BEST TRICK	1
SUMMER 1999	VERT DOUBLES	1
SUMMER 1998	VERT	3
SUMMER 1998	VERT DOUBLES	1
SUMMER 1997	VERT	1
SUMMER 1997	VERT DOUBLES	1
SUMMER 1996	PARK/STREET	7
SUMMER 1996	VERT	2
SUMMER 1995	PARK/STREET	2
SUMMER 1995	VERT	1

BIBLIOGRAPHY

Brooke, Michael. *The Concrete Wave: The History of Skateboarding.* Toronto: Warwick Publishing, 1999.

Cassorla, Albert. *The Ultimate Skateboard Book.* Philadelphia: Running Press, 1988.

Christopher, Matt. *On the Halfpipe with . . . Tony Hawk.* New York: Little, Brown and Company, 2001.

Hawk, Tony. *Hawk: Occupation: Skateboarder.* New York: ReganBooks, an imprint of HarperCollins Publishers, 2000.

Maikels, Terrence (editor). *Thrasher: Insane Terrain.* New York: Universe Publishing, 2001.

Pittman, Steve. *Tony Hawk: Chairman of the Board.* New York: Scholastic Inc., 2001.

Newspaper and Magazine Articles

Edgers, Geoff. "Hawk Hot as a Firecracker." *Toronto Star,* June 20, 2002.

"Flyboy." *People,* January 8, 2001.

Gordon, Devin. "Tony Hawk." *Newsweek,* October 14, 2002.

Keteyian, Armen. "Chairman of the Board." *Sports Illustrated,* November 24, 1986.

Layden, Tim. "Making Millions." *Sports Illustrated,* June 10, 2002, vol. 96, issue 24.

Levine, Mark. "The Birdman." *The New Yorker,* July 26, 1999.

Luna, Christopher. "Tony Hawk." *Current Biography,* June 2002.

Mandatory Information. *Transworld Skateboarding,* June 2002, vol. 20, issue 6.

Mandatory Information. *Transworld Skateboarding,* December 2001, vol. 19, issue 12.

Mendelsohn, Aline. "Officially Retired, Champion Skateboarder Tony Hawk Keeps Busy." *Orlando Sentinel,* January 21, 2002.

Mortimer, Sean. "Chairman of the Board." *Sports Illustrated for Kids,* July 1998, vol. 10, issue 7.

Mortimer, Sean. "Giving It Away." *Transworld Skateboarding Business* (online), September 26, 2002.

Mortimer, Sean. "Tony Hawk." *Parks & Recreation,* July 1999.

Pryor, Matthew. "Matthew Pryor Shapes Up With . . .Tony Hawk," *The Times,* February 17, 2001.

Ruibal, Sal. "Hawk's Success Soars Beyond Skateboard." *USA Today,* June 22, 1998.

Ruibal, Sal. "Next Wave of Athletes Gets Early Start." *USA Today,* August 19, 2002.

Wood, Daniel B. "No Fear of Flying—or Falling." *Christian Science Monitor,* December 30, 1986.

"Working the Streets." *Rolling Stone,* April 30, 1998, issue 785.

"X-Treme Profits." *Fortune,* March 4, 2002.

Zolecki, Todd. "Hawk Steals Show at X Games." *Philadelphia Inquirer,* August 19, 2001.

Zorianna, Kit. "Revolution Rolls With Skater Hawk." *Hollywood Reporter,* August 28, 2001, vol. 369, issue 39.

WEB SITES

ABC Online

http://www.abc.net.au/triplej/sport/features/hawk.htm

Official site of the Australian Broadcasting Company

Club Tony Hawk

http://www.clubtonyhawk.com

A members-only fan club site, full of information about the skater. Membership is free and includes access to the site.

CNNSI.com

http://sportsillustrated.cnn.com

Official site of the famous sports magazine

DeadSeriousSports.com

http://www.deadserioussports.com

Web site dedicated to extreme sports action, including skate-boarding and motocross

EXPN

http://expn.go.com/athletes/bios/HAWK_TONY.html

Official site of EXPN

Gravity Games

http://www.gravitygames.com

Features and information on NBC's extreme sporting event

Skateboard

http://www.extremesports.gr/skateboard/

Skateboarding site, including tips, tricks, and links

Tony Hawk Foundation

http://www.tonyhawkfoundation.org

The Tony Hawk Foundation issues grants and makes charitable donations for the creation of public skateboard parks, among other causes. The site has information on how to build a skate park and grant applications.

Tony Hawk's Boom Boom Huckjam

http://www.boomboomhuckjam.com

The official site of the live-action sports event, featuring links to reviews and video clips of the show

Transworld Skateboarding

http://www.skateboarding.com/skate/

Official site of the skateboarding magazine, offering many articles in printable text format

FILMOGRAPHY

The Making of Tony Hawk's Boom Boom Huckjam
(2002) . . . Himself

Jackass: The Movie (2002) . . . Himself

XXX (2002) . . . Xander's friend

The New Guy (2002) . . . Himself

Haggard (2002) . . . Officer

Max Keeble's Big Move (2001) . . . Himself

Extreme Air 2001 (2001) TV Series . . . Himself

Dogtown and Z-Boys (2001) . . . Himself

2000 Billboard Music Awards (2000) (TV) . . . Himself

The End (2000) . . . Himself

Gleaming the Cube (1989) . . . Buddy

Police Academy 4: Citizens on Patrol (1987) . . . Skateboarder

Thrashin' (1986) . . . Pool skater

INDEX